P9-EDX-866

# Weight Training

**By John Lear**

National & Olympic Weightlifting Coach



Published in collaboration with the
British Amateur Weight Lifters' Association

**Contents**

# Foreword

Training for strength must be one of the oldest activities known to man. The strong and the athletic were admired within early societies and the young would try to emulate them. Special contests were held, initially many of a primitive nature; but soon the idea was developed that success could come from training. Competition became more intense and sophisticated, eventually leading to such events as the early Olympic Games. Now that there were great honours to be won, athletes and trainers experimented to find new ways of improving their standards. The part played by strength in a wide range of sports activities was soon recognised.

Other sections of society also made demands on the fit and strong. Warfare demanded an ability to handle heavy weapons and shields, to march for great distances carrying all one's personal equipment and at the end to fight and win. The military looked for ways of developing and strengthening their men, and resistance training played its part.

Weight training as we know it today really begins with the strong men of the end of the last century, such men as Sandow, the Saxon Brothers and the immortal George Hackenschmidt. These men were very strong, but their strength was not a gift of birth as the public imagined: it was the result of hard training very similar in content to the methods and exercises followed by the modern weight trainer.

Another spur to sports weight training came during the last war. The Ack-Ack Command had introduced a new high-speed mechanical loader for their gun, but found to their horror that the gun crews were not strong enough to keep the loader supplied with heavy shells. Al Murray was called in to find an answer and devised special training, using the shells for a six-week period. At the end of it the crews were more than able to match the loader's appetite. This demonstration of progressive resistance training was witnessed by many members of the Physical Training Corps, and its values and application could be seen for other activities. After the war Al Murray was appointed first National Coach to the British Amateur Weight Lifters' Association, and he, together with Oscar State, began to draw up schedules of training for various sports. The first to recognise their value was Geof Dyson, National Coach to the A.A.A., soon to be followed by Bert Kinnear from the Amateur Swimming Association. Weight training was recognised as an essential part of athletic training.

Al Murray has continued to develop the use of resistance training and is now the world's leading authority on its use in medical rehabilitation and fitness training.

One of the most popular places at the Montreal Olympic Games was the weight-training room where one could see both men and women athletes, from all sports, training on the barbells, dumb-bells and the new weight-training machines. Some of the field athletes even went down to the weightlifting hall to train on the heavier apparatus with the weightlifters.

I hope that in reading this book you will find real assistance for your activity and that it will help you to become more successful and fulfil your true potential.

JOHN LEAR
*National and Olympic Coach*
*British Amateur Weight Lifters' Association*

# Introduction

Weight Training or Progressive Resistance Exercise is now an integral part of all modern sports preparation. There are real advantages to be obtained in this form of training. It may take many forms and use various apparatus, some complicated and some simple. This book will deal with the simplest and still the most effective form, using weights via barbells and dumb-bells and the popular weight-training machines now to be found in most sports centres.

The methods described are based on progression with the resistance handled. All too often one comes across training plans, which include schedules, where the needs of the athlete have not been fully understood. The general and specific requirements of the event and the time of the year or season are covered, blanket fashion, often with complicated exercises and extended workouts, more suited to the competitive weightlifter or bodybuilder. The weight trainer is neither of these. His objective is to improve his sport, and so for him weight training is an assistance only. Coaches who are concerned with this form of training should study the anatomy and kinetics of the event so that they can teach the proper exercises. Then they would not waste time with work that can be either useless or harmful in that it strengthens groups of muscles not involved or even antagonistic to those used in the event.

The sports man or woman is advised to study the book carefully—especially the exercise photographs and descriptions—and to perform the recommended movements using the strictest possible exercise techniques at all times. Remember that poor exercise technique could lead to injury resulting in restricted progress in your activity and a bad name for weight training. Do not increase the resistance at the expense of good technique. If you cannot perform the exercise properly then the weight that you are handling is too heavy.

Whenever possible, try to join a good weightlifting club or attend a sports centre where there is a qualified coach. The increase in strength and power will enable you to master skills with greater ease, to increase your speed and improve your ability to overcome resistance. The objective of this book is to help you gain success.

# 1. WEIGHT TRAINING FOR SPORT



## Basic Objectives

The use of weight training for sport has two main objectives. These are:

### 1. For All Major Games and Team Sports

- It forms a part of the general build-up of fitness and endurance, as related specifically to the period of play and to the rapid recovery from the physical stress of this time of activity. It also ensures the general ability to successfully complete the training plans presented during the week, or as required for competitions.
- It is used to develop power in the form of strength and speed training to enable a player to master, with ease, the essential skills of the game. Often skill will be limited to a low level, because the participant does not have the basic strength and power necessary for the mastery of the skill. Closely related to this is mobility, which can be developed and maintained. The strengthening of a muscle over its full range of movement is an essential aspect of a fitness programme.
- The developing and strengthening of muscles and ligaments will result in the minimisation of joint injury, and the more rapid rehabilitation of previously injured joints to full playing capacity.

## 2. Individual Sports

- It caters for demands for specific strength, speed and power training related to the special skills of these activities. This group will include all forms of athletics, swimming, boxing, wrestling, gymnastics, rowing etc., and those activities where levels of high personal ability are essential in obtaining success. Obviously the type of training with weights will vary from activity to activity. The work done by the heavy field athlete, such as the shot putter, will vary in approach from that followed by the long-distance runner.

Weight training therefore can be used to produce a variety of objectives. These are: (1) fitness of a general nature; (2) specific endurance; (3) strength and power; (4) speed. In order to achieve success these qualities must exist to a lesser or greater degree in all activities.

# Specific Objectives

## 1. Fitness

The types of exercises used in the fitness programme are those which employ large groups of muscles at one time. The objective is to place great overload on the cardio-vascular system—such exercises would include Power Cleaning and Snatching, High Pull-ups, Squats, Lunges and Bench Pressing. All these exercises are of a massive nature.

The repetitions must be high. A resistance is chosen that will permit ten repetitions without the loss of form. As the participant finds it easier to perform the ten repetitions, so he progresses to fifteen and from there to twenty in easy stages. When the selected maximum is achieved, the weight is increased so that he can now only perform ten repetitions. Again he works up until he can achieve the required maximum.

Rest pauses between sets of repetitions and between exercises should be kept to the minimum. These pauses should only be long enough to permit the breathing to return almost to normal. By almost to normal is meant to a level which will not affect the skill or rhythm of the movement or exercise. This in actual time is usually between thirty and ninety seconds maximum, depending upon the number of repetitions performed and the resistance used. Try to cut down on the length of the rest periods, so that greater demands are made on the cardio-vascular system.

## 2. Endurance

Endurance training is an extension of fitness work. The repetitions can be considerably increased up to as many as fifty. The exercises chosen should still be of a massive nature involving large muscle group complexes. The weights used will be light, and high repetitions will be performed quickly, with as short a rest period between the exercises and sets as possible.

## 3. Strength and Power Training

When we train for strength and power, we adopt the opposite procedure to that employed in fitness and endurance training, for now we need to use much heavier resistance with consequently lower repetitions. The resistance selected should not permit more than five repetitions to be performed for any exercise, and the total number of repetitions should not exceed twenty-five. An exercise could therefore be performed for five sets of five repetitions. At times it may be necessary to handle weights which permit only three or two repetitions, and the athlete may well go to singles, where maximum resistance is being handled. Exercises such as Power Cleans, High Pull-ups and Power Snatch, Upward Jumps with heavy weights, Heave Presses and Jerks with barbells and dumb-bells, Cheating Single-arm Rowing etc., are all good power exercises.

### 4. Speed

Successful speed training is dependent on increases in strength and power, for the athlete should have greater power than his activity limits demand. The shot putter requires far greater power and speed than the actual resistance that the 16 lb. (7 kg.) shot presents, and the soccer player requires very much greater speed and power of leg extension/flexion to kick a ball with effect than its limited weight presents. These reserves will enable them to overcome with far greater ease the resistance that a speed event places upon them.

## Sports Requirements Analysis

Here are examples of the requirements of three different sports.

### Soccer

Stop/start acceleration
Rapid and controlled change of direction
Springing and leaping
Kicking/shooting with both feet, with power
Ability to resist tackles, and thereby successfully complete skills and skilled moves
Specific power building for throwing, heading etc.
Prevention of injury through power/mobility training and rehabilitation of injuries to full playing capacity

### Shot Putting

Great skill } under resistance
High level of co-ordination } conditions
Very rapid acceleration
Abundant strength
Explosive power

### Rowing

Great skill } Under resistance
High level of co-ordination } conditions
Endurance
Power/acceleration
Power balance throughout the crew

Similar essential basic needs are to be found in all sports. Analyse your sport for its own special demands. A carefully prepared programme of weight training will help to ensure more successful participation.

## Planning the Weight Training Programme

The requirements for the various parts of the year will differ. The athlete and coach need to appreciate that the weight-training plans and schedules have different values depending upon the general training load placed upon the individual and the time of the competitive season.

The programme can broadly be divided into the following sections: (1) closed or non-playing phase; (2) pre-season phase; (3) start of season; (4) the full season.

### 1. The Closed or Non-playing Phase

The best time to introduce weight training to the athlete is during the non-playing period of the year. This will give him the opportunity to follow a comprehensive schedule which will lay down a basis of all-body fitness, mobility and strength. The schedule will be general, employing exercises for all muscle groups. The repetitions will be high so that adequate stress will be placed on the cardio-vascular system, and the resistance principle will be directed primarily to the increase of repetitions. This period should last from three to six weeks, and there should be three training sessions per week. In the initial stages the resistance will be only token, but towards the end of this period one should have a very good idea of the weights that can be handled in subsequent training phases.



### 2. Pre-Season Phase

For some four to eight weeks prior to the start of the season the number of exercises will be cut down and those of a massive nature employed. The resistance is increased with a corresponding reduction in the number of repetitions. The Set System is now employed. Training at this time becomes specific in laying down strength and power. Again you should train three times per week. This period should lead into . . .

### 3. Start of Season Phase

During this period, for about four weeks, a schedule directed to power building should be employed. Again the exercises are of a massive nature, but now attempts can be made at maxima. This means that an exercise can be followed on the repetition basis of 5-4-3-2-1-1. When a number of sets and repetitions is decided upon then there will be an increase in the poundage handled in each set. For example one set of repetitions of 50 lb. (22·5 kg.); one set of repetitions of 75 lb. (34 kg.), and one set of repetitions of 100 lb. (45 kg.). When the season has begun and the demands of the sport have increased, this period and the subsequent phase will involve training on two days per week only.

### 4. The Full Season

Once the season is in full swing, the objective is to maintain the basis of power that has been developed in the previous training periods. Again the training will

## Example of a Training Plan for a Games Player

| *Closed Season* | *Pre-Season* | *Start of Season* | *Throughout Season* |
|---|---|---|---|
| Learning fitness, mobility<br>High pulse rate—short rest | Strength build up | Power build up | Power maintenance |
| 3 times per week<br>Mon. Wed. Fri. | 3 times per week<br>Mon. Wed Fri. | 2 times per week<br>Mon. Wed. | 2 times per week<br>Mon. Wed. |
| High Pull Up 2 sets 10-20 reps.<br>Press Behind Neck 2 sets 10-20 reps.<br>2 Hands Curl 2 sets 10-20 reps.<br>D/B Side Bend 2 sets 10-20 reps.<br><br>Bent Forward Rowing 2 sets 10-20 reps.<br>Back Squat 2 sets 10-20 reps.<br><br>Power Cleans 2 sets 10-20 reps.<br><br>Bench Press 2 sets 10-20 reps.<br>Pullovers 2 sets 10-20 reps.<br>bdominals 2 sets 10-30 reps. | Power Cleans 4 sets 8 reps.<br>Heave Press 4 sets 8 reps.<br>Back Squats 4 sets 8 reps.<br>Twisting 1 arm Rowing 4 sets 8 reps.<br><br>*Lunges 4 sets 10 reps. (each leg)<br>Abdominals (with weights) 4 sets 10 reps. | Power Cleans 5-4-3-2-1-1<br>Heave Press 5-4-3-2-1-1<br>Squat Jumps 3 sets 5 reps.<br>Dead Lift 3 sets 5 reps.<br><br>Side Bends 2 sets 8 reps. | *Schedule 'A' Monday*<br>Power Cleans 5 sets 4 reps.<br>Heave Press 5 sets 4 reps.<br>Twisting 1 arm Rowing 5 sets 4 reps.<br><br>*Lunges 5 sets 6 reps. (each leg)<br><br>*Schedule 'B' Wednesdays*<br>High Pulls (wide grip) 5 sets 4 reps.<br>Squat Jumps 5 sets 4 reps.<br>Power Cleans 5 sets 4 reps.<br>*Lunges 5 sets 6 reps. (each leg) |
| 6 weeks depending on<br>sting level of fitness | 4-8 weeks | 4 weeks | Remaining playing time |

pecific exercises
ecific exercises for other sports should be introduced during pre-season onwards. They will replace the illustrated example marked *
may be included as is found to be necessary.

be on two days per week. Select good general power exercises and a resistance sufficient to ensure that the repetitions are kept low, and then perform five sets of each exercise. This type of training can be followed throughout the season with good results as far as the maintenance of power is concerned. Since the use of weights is challenging in itself, do not be afraid to increase the poundage handled, providing that correct lifting technique is maintained at all times.

The more advanced field athletes using shot, discus, hammer and javelin generally follow very much heavier weight-training programmes than those laid out in this book. Such individuals are strongly advised to join a weightlifting club, where there will be facilities, coaching and apparatus that will cater for their needs.

### Selection of Weight to be Handled

Because there are differences in the physical build of all individuals, it is not possible to be definite about the weight to be used. This will be decided by the athlete or his or her coach after the initial training period. To start with, a weight must be selected that will enable movements to be learnt and yet thoroughly exercise the participant. Weights in the range of 15 to 30 lb. (7-14 kg.) will be suitable depending upon the individual. You may find these to be very light, but remember that you have to work up to twenty repetitions and learn all the exercises. In subsequent training periods, weights can be adjusted to your own developing strength levels.

### Sets and Repetitions

The amount of work that one requires to do is broken up into sets of a required number of repetitions. For example, if a lifter decides that he needs to perform thirty repetitions of an exercise, his choice lies between the development of endurance or strength. For endurance he might complete the thirty repetitions in one set without any rest. This would mean that the weight would have to be light. On the other hand, as one of the main objectives of weightlifting training is to develop strength, the resistance handled must be increased. Now he cannot perform one set of thirty, so the exercise is performed over three sets of ten repetitions or six sets of five. At more advanced levels, when the resistance is very heavy, he performs ten sets of three. This is known as the Set System of training.

### Warming up

Before any weight training it is essential that you follow a short warm-up period of free-standing exercises. These are those that you will have lear whilst at school, and should include full- mobility work for all the major joint complexes body.

## Weight Training Machines

These are now very popular and are found sports centres. The machines are made up c stations, the weight trainer moving from s station performing his exercises. Some specific

Weight
Training
Machine

cannot be performed on these machines, so traditional barbell exercises may have to be used as well.

The basic training principles are the same as for other forms of weight training.

## Schedules for Use with Weight Training Machines

### Programme 1
### Non-Playing/Competitive Season

**Objectives**

General fitness, mobility, basic strengthening

**Methods**

Resistance training, short rests between sets and exercises, high pulse

Three sessions per week

Free-standing warm up; mobilising exercises for all joint complexes

| | | | | |
|---|---|---|---|---|
| Press behind neck | 2 | sets of | 10 | repetitions |
| Upright rowing | 2 | ,, ,, | 10 | ,, |
| Side bends (both sides) | 2 | ,, ,, | 10 | ,, |
| Two hands curl (not for ladies) | 2 | ,, ,, | 10 | ,, |
| Press on back | 2 | ,, ,, | 10 | ,, |
| Leg press | 2 | ,, ,, | 10 | ,, |
| Pull-downs (standing) | 2 | ,, ,, | 10 | ,, |
| Abdominal work (sit-ups on the flat floor) | 2 | ,, ,, | 10 | ,, |

Light free-standing exercise to finish

This schedule should be followed for six to eight weeks. Select a resistance that ensures really hard work for the last few repetitions of each set but *withou losing exercise form.* Resistance can be increase as the participant feels able, but bearing the abov important exercise criteria in mind at all times.

### Programme 2
### Pre-Season/Start of Season

**Objectives**

Power build up

**Methods**

Resistance training, increased resistance/sets

Three sessions per week

Free-standing warm up; mobilising exercises for a joint complexes

| | | | | |
|---|---|---|---|---|
| Seated press (facing station) | 3 | sets of | 8 | repetitio |
| Bent forward rowing | 3 | ,, ,, | 8 | ,, |
| Side bends (both sides) | 3 | ,, ,, | 8 | ,, |
| Press on back | 3 | ,, ,, | 8 | ,, |
| Leg press | 3 | ,, ,, | 8 | ,, |
| Pull-downs (kneeling) | 3 | ,, ,, | 8 | ,, |
| Abdominal work | 3 | ,, ,, | 10 | ,, |

Light free-standing exercise to finish

This schedule should be followed for four to s weeks. After the completion of Programme 1, t participant will have a very good idea of the measure the resistance that can be handled, bearing in mind t principles of strict exercise technique. Keep the r periods between exercises and sets short—abc ninety seconds maximum.

**Programme 3**
**Throughout Playing Season**
**Objectives**
Power maintenance

## Methods

Resistance training; increased resistance leading to increased number of sets but with lower number of repetitions in each set

Two sessions per week

Free-standing warm up; mobilising exercises for all joint complexes

| | |
|---|---|
| Seated press behind neck | 5 sets of 5 repetitions |
| Upright rowing | 5 ,, ,, 5 ,, |
| Press on back | 5 ,, ,, 5 ,, |
| Leg press | 5 ,, ,, 5 ,, |
| Pull-downs (kneeling) | 5 ,, ,, 5 ,, |

Abdominal work; alternate each session, as follows: 'V' sit-ups (fast movement on floor) or sit-ups on inclined board

Light free-standing exercise to finish

This schedule can be followed through the playing season and should be undertaken twice per week. Try to arrange your workouts so that they do not take place on the days of, or immediately prior to, the day of major competition.

## General Exercises

These are all exercises which affect the major muscle groups of the body. These exercises also throw great demand on the cardio-vascular system. Eventually you should expect to handle heavy resistance through these movements. They develop great power and determination.

## Specific Exercises

Many athletic events are very specialised in their movements and will require special weight-training exercises. Consult a coach of the event and study the mechanics, anatomy and kinetics of the movement. Look at the action. It can most certainly be divided into three main sections:

1. Arms and shoulders
2. Trunk action
3. Leg action

By studying the movement in this way you will be able to find in which part of the movement the greatest force is exerted. This will give you the line of the force and the angle of the body when the force is applied. In performing the specific weight-training exercise the body must be placed so that the line of force will be vertical. So the inclined Dumb-bell Press is used for the shot putter (see *Fig. A*, page 14).

The same principle is applied to other sports, though the angle of force may be upwards, downwards, diagonal or horizontal. In free-style swimming, for example, the force is downwards against the resistance of the water (*Fig. B*, page 14). Unless you employ pulley work to achieve a downward movement the body must be placed so that the movement with weights is in fact upwards. Hence the use of the Declined Straight-arm Pull-over.

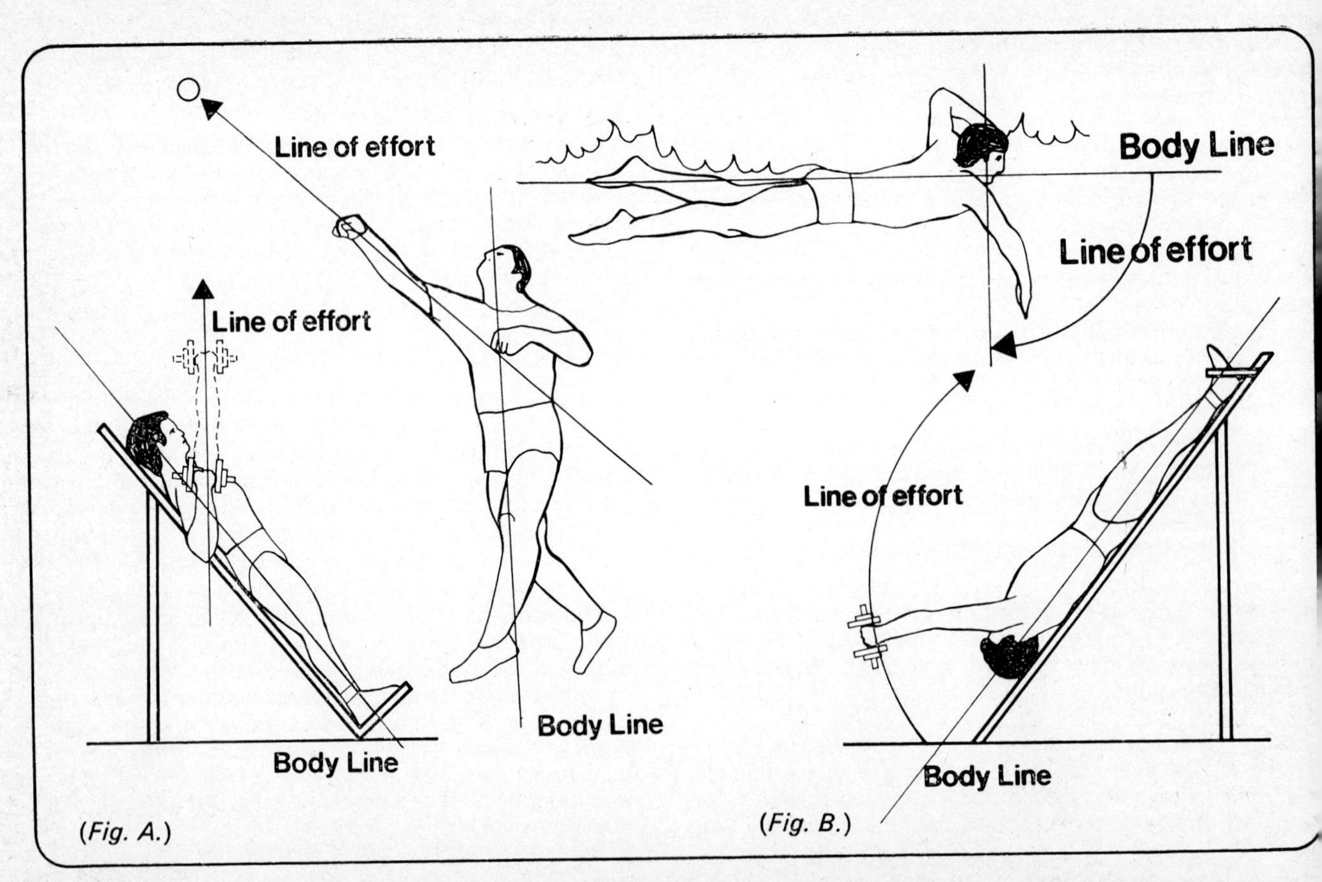
Line of effort
Line of effort
Body Line
Body Line
Body Line
Line of effort
Line of effort
Body Line
(Fig. A.)
(Fig. B.)

**Select Exercises According to Sport and Include in Schedule**

| Sport | Exercises |
|---|---|
| **Sprinting** | Squat Jumps<br>Step-ups with weights |
| **Shot** | Bench Press and inclined Bench Press |
| **Discus** | Bench Press and Lateral Raise Lying |
| **Javelin** | Bench Press and Pull-over exercises |
| **Hammer** | Squat Jumps; Bench Press |
| **Jumping** | Squat Jumps<br>Step-ups with weights<br>Abdominal work<br>Leg raising with weighted boots |
| **Pole vault** | Abdominal work<br>Pulling and Cleaning movements<br>Bench Press |
| **Swimming** | Declined Pull-overs<br>Lateral Raise Lying<br>Pulley work |
| **Tennis, Squash and Badminton** | Lunges<br>Twisting Single Arm Rowing for trunk and backhand play<br>Lateral Raise Lying |
| **Major Team Games** | Lunges<br>Trunk work |
| **Rowing and Canoeing** | Squat Jumps<br>Power Cleans<br>Bent Forward Rowing |
| **Gymnastics** | Abdominal work<br>Arm and shoulder exercises |
| **Wrestling** | Power Cleaning<br>Wrestler's Bridge |
| **Judo** | Power Cleaning |
| **Boxing** | Inclined Alternate Dumb-bell Pressing |
| **Archery and Shooting** | Exercises to develop arm and shoulder strength for control |
| **Fencing** | Lunges |

Other activities will benefit from general weight training.

Where there is a choice given of more than one exercise, different movements can be selected to be included in separate days' workouts.

## 2. THE EXERCISES

### The High Pull-up

**Starting Position** Assume starting position. Get Set. (*Fig. A.*)

**Movement** Pull the bar high. Note the position of the wrists and elbow, also the position of the chest—it is high and the hips are slightly forward as the body comes up high on the toes. Repeat in a brisk, non-stop rhythm. (*Fig. B.*)

**Breathing** Breathe in as you raise the bar, and out as you lower to the starting position.

**Purpose** With light weights this movement is useful as a warming-up exercise. However, with heavier weights it is a real all-round power builder.

(*Fig. B.*)

(*Fig. A.*)

## Press behind Neck

**Starting Position** Feet astride with the bar resting comfortably behind the neck. (*Fig. A.*)

**Movement** Press the barbell straight to arms' length overhead. (*Fig. B.*)

**Breathing** Breathe in on the upward movement and out as you return to starting position.

**Purpose** To develop the upper back muscles, muscles of the shoulder and those at the rear of the upper arm.

(*Fig. A.*) (*Fig. B.*)

## Two Hands Curl

**Starting Position** Note that the body is vertical, arms straight and palms to the front. (*Fig. A.*)

**Movement** Bend the arms strongly at the elbows until the bar rests on the chest. Make sure that the bar is kept close to the body. (*Fig. B.*)

**Finishing Position** Note that the elbows are fully flexed, yet still behind the bar, thus keeping the resistance on the muscles concerned. Should you bring the elbows forward and upwards, you will take all the resistance away and defeat the object of the exercise.

By varying the grip on the bar from a wide grip to a very close one, or by changing the position of the trunk, the effect of the exercise can be altered.

**Breathing** Breathe in as you raise the bar and out as you lower it.

**Purpose** To develop the muscle on the front of the upper arm.

(*Fig. A.*) (*Fig. B.*)

## Power Cleans with Barbell

**Starting Position** The legs are well bent but the back is flat. (*Fig. A.*)

**Movement** Extend the legs and back vigorously, bringing the arms into action as the barbell passes the mid thighs, finishing in the receiving position. (*Fig. B.*)

**Breathing** Breathe in as you lift and out as you lower the barbell to the starting position.

**Purpose** To develop all-round body power. This exercise can also be done with dumb-bells.

(*Fig. B.*)

(*Fig. A.*)

## Upright Rowing

**Starting Position** Bend down, grip the bar, knuckles to the front, hands approximately 8 in. apart and stand up. The bar should now be hanging at arms' length against the top of the thighs. This is the starting position. (*Fig. A.*)

**Movement** Pull the bar up the front of the body until it reaches the height of the chin. (*Fig. B.*)

**Breathing** Breathe in as the bar is raised and out as you return it to the starting position.

**Purpose** To develop the muscles surrounding the shoulders and upper back, also the muscle which flexes the elbow.

**Variation** In a cheating version, the legs may be used slightly to assist the exerciser to handle heavier weights.

(*Fig. B.*)

(*Fig. A.*)

## Bent-Forward Rowing

**Starting Position** The back is flat, head up, arms straight, knuckles to the front, hands fairly wide apart, feet wide astride, knees slightly bent. (*Fig. A.*)

**Movement** Pull the bar strongly to the chest, by bending the arms and raising the elbows sideways. Lower barbell under control. (*Fig. B.*)

**Raised Position** This shows the position as the bar touches the top of the chest. It is excellent exercise for improving shoulder posture. Note that the body has not moved during the movement.

**Breathing** Breathe in as the bar is pulled to the chest, and out as the weight is returned to the starting position.

**Purpose** Principally to develop the upper back muscles. The effects of this exercise can be altered by bringing the bar up and back to touch the lower abdomen. This affects the lower back muscles.

(*Fig. B.*)

(*Fig. A.*)

## The Squat (or Full Knee Bend)

**Starting Position** Feet are comfortably apart, normally hip width, with the bar resting across the upper back. (The heels may be raised on blocks of wood $1\frac{1}{2}$ in. high.) (*Fig. A.*)

**Movement** Bend the knees and squat down, gently rebound out of the low position and rise strongly by lifting the head, at the same time strongly straightening the legs. (*Fig. B.*)

**Low Position** The back is flat, but not vertical. This position elevates the ribs and has a stretching effect on the thorax, which encourages chest growth. The Squat can be used with many variations for the legs, or as a general power builder. Due to the larger groups of muscles being used, a great demand is made on the circulatory and respiratory systems, which greatly encourages increasing body weight. The Squat is the keystone of many weight-training schedules. Should you find difficulty in keeping the back flat as you approach the low position, it is advisable either to avoid going all the way down or to put a chock of wood under the heels about $1\frac{1}{2}$ in. high. This throws most of the resistance on the front of the thighs.

The effects of this exercise can be greatly altered by the extent to which the exerciser bends his legs. Several hundred pounds can be used in shallow or half squats.

**Breathing** Fill the lungs, bend the knees, breathe out just as you rebound in the low position and you will find that the air is driven out of the lungs. Breathe in as you rise.

**Purpose** To develop the legs, back and chest, and to improve the condition of the heart and lungs. *Note:* in most cases it is neither necessary nor advisable to go lower than in the illustrated position.

**Vertical or Squat Jumps** From a half squat position leap upwards, putting as much effort as possible into the drive from the legs. Be sure to land on the toes. Bend the knees to take the shock out of landing. Make sure you are well balanced before each repetition. This variation develops an explosive leg action and also develops the muscles of the hips, front of thighs and calf muscles.

(*Fig. A.*) (*Fig. B.*)

## Front Squats

**Starting Position** Feet are comfortably apart, normally hip width, with the bar resting across the upper chest. (*Fig. A.*)

**Movement** Lower the body into the full squat position. (*Fig. B.*) Vigorously extend the legs and return to the upright standing position.

**Breathing** Breathe out as you bend the knees and in as you rise to the standing position.

**Purpose** To develop mainly the muscles on the front of the thighs and the hip muscles.

(*Fig. A.*) (*Fig. B.*)

## Lunges or Split Squats

**Starting Position** Take up the position illustrated, front leg stepped well forward, rear foot pointing straight ahead, heel raised, bar held high on the chest. Make sure that your balance is perfect before attempting the movement. (*Fig. A.*)

**Movement** Lower the body and the weight from this position by bending both legs. (*Fig. B.*) Note that the forward knee should be in advance of the forward foot. The direction of the lunge can be altered with each repetition, as can the leading leg. For example, first repetition directly forward, recover feet together, changing leading leg, lunge to side, recover feet together, changing leading leg, lunge to opposite side, and so on.

**Breathing** Breathe as freely as possible during the exercise.

**Purpose** To build power and mobility in the legs. This exercise is especially valuable to all racket games players.

(*Fig. A.*)

(*Fig. B.*)

## Heave Press

**Starting Position** Pull the barbell from the floor to the chest, dip the body by bending the legs and assume the starting position. (*Fig. A.*)

**Movement** Extend the legs and arms vigorously; finish the last half of the movement in the correct pressing style. (*Fig. B.*)

**Breathing** Breathe in as you extend the arms and legs and as you lower the bar to the starting position. As this is a power movement, it is often necessary to breathe in and out a few times between repetitions at the shoulder.

**Purpose** To produce collectively power and development in the arms, shoulders and legs. Muscles: The extensors of the arms and legs; the shoulder flexors and elevators of the shoulder girdle. This exercise can also be performed with dumb-bells.

(*Fig. A.*) (*Fig. B.*)

## Straight-legged Dead Lift

**Starting Position** Feet hip width apart, arms straight and chest held high. (*Fig. A.*)

**Movement** Round the spine and bend forward from the hips until your barbell touches the ground. In the early stages, the knees can be very slightly bent. (*Fig. B.*)

**Low Position** When this exercise is performed correctly with a light weight it adds greatly to the mobility of the spine. When lowering from the starting position, begin by lowering the head first, followed by rounding the shoulders and upper back. In other words, make sure you round the spine as a whole. When recovering, attempt to straighten up the lower spine first: the head should be the last part to be raised to the erect position. It is advisable to progress slowly with this particular exercise.

**Breathing** Breathe out as you lower the bar, and in as you return the bar to the starting position.

**Purpose** To develop the muscles which extend the spine and hip joints, the hip muscles and the hamstring group at the back of the upper leg.

**Variation** The above exercise can be performed with a flat back and feet astride. This throws all the resistance on to the lower back, hip and hamstrings (muscles behind the thigh).

(*Fig. A.*) (*Fig. B.*)

## Press on Bench

**Starting Position** Back-lying, on bench. Bar resting on the chest, fore-arms vertical below the bar, hands wide apart. (*Fig. A.*)

**Movement** Press the barbell vigorously to arms' length. (*Fig. B.*)

**Breathing** Breathe in as you press the bar upwards and out as you return it to the chest.

**Purpose** To develop the chest muscles, front shoulder muscles and muscles on the back of the upper arm.

**Variation** This exercise can be performed by supporting the bar across the lower chest, hands shoulder-width apart, arms close to the side of the chest. This variation throws a greater resistance on the arms and shoulders.

(*Fig. A.*)

(*Fig. B.*)

## Trunk Forward Bend

**Starting Position** Assume feet-astride position with the bar resting comfortably behind the neck. (*Fig. A.*)

**Movement** Bend forwards from the hips, keeping the back flat, but allow the knees to bend slightly as the trunk comes horizontal to the ground. (*Fig. B.*)

**Breathing** Breathe out as you bend forwards and in as you return to the starting position.

**Purpose** To develop the muscles at the rear of thigh, hips and the lower back muscles.

(*Fig. A.*) (*Fig. B.*)

## Dumb-bell Side to Side Bend

**Starting Position** Stand astride a dumb-bell, bend down and pick it up with the right hand, and assume the illustrated starting position. (*Fig. A.*) Keep the body square to the front.

**Movement** Bend the body strongly to the left as far as possible. (*Fig. B.*)

**Finishing Position** Note how the body has kept to the lateral plane.

**Breathing** Breathe in as you raise the weight and out as you return to the starting position.

**Purpose** To develop the muscles on the sides of the trunk and numerous other muscles surrounding the mid-section.

(*Fig. A.*) (*Fig. B.*)

## Cheating Single-arm Rowing

**Starting Position** Take up position, keeping the back as flat as possible. (*Fig. A.*)

**Movement** Pull the dumb-bell vigorously up into position. (*Fig. B.*) Rotate the trunk so that the chest is facing sideways and upwards. Keep the free hand on a low chair or stool. This should not be higher than 1ft. (0.3 m) above the floor.

**Breathing** Breathe in as you raise the dumb-bell and out as you return to the starting position.

**Purpose** To develop the muscles which rotate the trunk, also those of the shoulder and upper back.

(*Fig. B.*)

(*Fig. A.*)

## Straight-arm Pull-over

**Starting Position** Back-lying on a narrow bench. The barbell is held at arms' length. (*Fig. A.*)

**Movement** Keep the arms straight and lower the bar in a quarter circle backwards until you reach the position shown in the illustration, or even lower down. (*Fig. B.*)

**Stretch Position** In the early stages, it is advisable to keep the lower back flat on the bench, and the weight light. A good point to remember in all straight-arm movements is the advisability of performing the first two repetitions in slow, steady time to make sure the muscles are stretched over the full range, before you attempt the exercise at full tempo.

**Breathing** Breathe in as you lower the bar, and out as you return to the starting position.

**Purpose** To enlarge the thorax and develop muscles surrounding the shoulder girdle, also the muscles on the front of the chest and the large muscles of the lower back.

**Variation** The bar may be started from a resting place across the thighs.

(*Fig. A.*)

(*Fig. B.*)

## Bent-arm Pull-over

**Starting Position** Back-lying on a bench or form, bar resting on the lower chest, but with narrow grip and elbows at the sides. (*Fig. A.*)

**Movement** Raise the bar off the chest and directly backwards over the head until it reaches the illustrated position. Try to keep the elbow joints at right angles throughout the movement. (*Fig. B.*)

**Breathing** Breathe in as the bar goes backwards, and out as you return the bar to the chest.

**Purpose** To stretch and mobilise the thorax, and to develop the chest muscles and the large muscles of the lower back.

**Variation** A centrally loaded dumb-bell may be used.

(*Fig. A.*)

(*Fig. B.*)

## Standing Tricep Press with Dumb-bell

**Starting Position** Feet astride with the dumb-bell lowered behind neck. (*Fig. A.*)

**Movement** Vigorously straighten the elbow until the dumb-bell is above the head. (*Fig. B.*)

**Breathing** Breathe in as the dumb-bell is raised, and out as it is lowered.

**Purpose** To develop the muscles at the rear of the upper arm.

(*Fig. A.*) (*Fig. B.*)

## Dumb-bell Press

**Starting Position** Grip two dumb-bells, one in each hand; bring the bells to the shoulders. (*Fig. A.*)

**Movement** Press the dumb-bell evenly to arms' length overhead, keeping the body in the starting position throughout. As you drive the bells from the shoulder, lift the chest high. (*Fig. B.*)

**Finishing Position** The chest is held high and the body is in a strong upright position with the elbows straight and the arms vertical. Dumb-bell work has a great strengthening effect on the muscles. This is especially true of the overhead exercises, as they are much more difficult to control than the barbell.

**Breathing** Breathe in as the bells are pressed overhead, and out as the bells are returned to the starting position.

**Purpose** To develop the shoulder muscles, upper back muscles and the muscle at the back of the upper arm.

(*Fig. A.*) (*Fig. B.*)

## Dumb-bell Screw Curl

**Starting Position** Stand erect, feet a few inches apart; dumb-bells hanging at arms' length with rear end of the disc pointing forward. (*Fig. A.*)

**Movement** Bend the arms strongly at the elbows; as the bells reach the midway position, turn the rear ends in towards each other. Keep the elbows from coming too far forwards at the completion of the curl. (*Fig. B.*)

**Finishing Position** The body is erect and the elbows are still behind the bells; this is important to keep the resistance on the muscles being used.

**Breathing** Breathe in as the weights are raised, and out as you return to the starting position.

**Purpose** To develop the muscles of the front of the upper arm.

(*Fig. A.*) (*Fig. B.*)

## Single-arm Rowing

**Starting Position** Feet astride, legs bent, one hand supported on a low bench. The dumb-bell hangs vertically beneath the shoulder. (*Fig. A.*)

**Movement** Pull the dumb-bell strongly from the starting position to a point close to the side of the chest. (*Fig. B.*)

**Breathing** Breathe in as the bell is raised, and out as you return to the starting position.

**Purpose** To develop the upper back muscles, the trunk and muscles on the front of the upper arm.

(*Fig. A.*)

(*Fig. B.*)

## Tricep Bench Press with Dumb-bells

**Starting Position** Back-lying, dumb-bells held as in the illustration. (*Fig. A.*) Note the backward angle of the arms and the tilt back of the bells. The bells are supported by the little finger side of the hand resting against the inside of the front disc.

**Movement** Keep the upper arm still as you lower the bells into a position behind the head. (*Fig. B.*) Drive the bells straight back to the starting position, making sure they never come vertically over the shoulders. This keeps the resistance on the triceps muscles.

**Lower Position** Care should be taken in lowering the bells from the raised position. Note the elbows are well bent and pointed high. The hands are close to the inside of the front discs.

**Breathing** Breathe in as the bells are raised, and out as they are lowered.

**Purpose** To develop the muscles at the back of the upper arm.

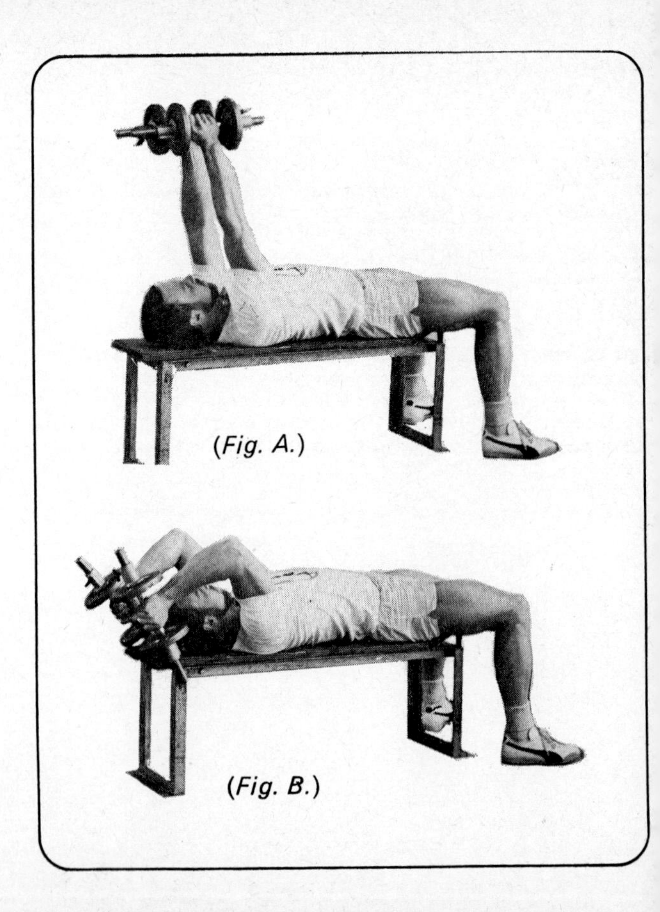

(*Fig. A.*)

(*Fig. B.*)

## Bent-forward Tricep Press with Dumb-bells

**Starting Position** Feet astride, knees bent. Lower the chest close to the upper thighs, elbows pointing upwards. (*Fig. A.*)

**Movement** Hold this position and extend both elbows. The body, and shoulders are to be kept still during the movement. (*Fig. B.*)

**Breathing** Breathe freely throughout the movement.

**Purpose** A very strong exercise to develop the muscles at the rear of the upper arm.

(*Fig. A.*)

(*Fig. B.*)

## Lateral Raise Lying

**Starting Position** Back-lying on a narrow bench or form. Dumb-bells are held at arms' length vertically over the shoulders. (*Fig. A.*)

**Movement** Keep the arms straight, lower the bells sideways until they are approximately below the level of the shoulders. Comparatively light weights must be used for this exercise. (*Fig. B.*)

**Breathing** Breathe in as the bells are lowered, and out as the bells are returned to the starting position.

**Purpose** To develop the chest muscles and muscles on the front of the shoulders.

(*Fig. A.*)

(*Fig. B.*)

## Lateral Raise Standing with Dumb-bells

**Starting Position** Assume the feet-astride position with the dumb-bells resting against the thighs. (*Fig. A.*)

**Movement** Raise the dumb-bells sideways. Raise the chest high at the same time. Lower and repeat the movement. (*Fig. B.*)

**Breathing** Breathe in as you raise the bells, and out as they return to the starting position.

**Purpose** To develop the shoulders and upper back muscles.

(*Fig. B.*)

(*Fig. A.*)

## Bent-forward Lateral Raise Standing

**Starting Position** Knees slightly bent, back flat, and horizontal to the ground. (*Fig. A.*)

**Movement** Maintain the starting position of back and legs and raise the dumb-bells sideways to a point slightly above the level of the shoulders. (*Fig. B.*)

**Breathing** Breathe in as you raise the bells, and out as you return to the starting position.

**Purpose** To develop the abductors of the scapulae and muscles which cap the shoulder joint.

(*Fig. B.*)

(*Fig. A.*)

# Forward Raise Standing

**Starting Position** Body upright, feet hip width apart, dumb-bells resting across the thighs. (*Fig. A.*)

**Movement** Keeping the arms straight, raise the dumb-bells forwards to a point slightly above the level of the shoulders. Keep the chest high throughout the movement. (*Fig. B.*)

**Breathing** Breathe in as the dumb-bells are raised, and out as you return to the starting position.

**Purpose** To develop the muscles of the front of the shoulders.

(*Fig. A.*) (*Fig. B.*)

## Weight-Training Safety

The use of weights as a means of developing strength and power is very old indeed. Weight training—i.e. strength and muscle building—is a very worthwhile end in itself. Strength is respectable. It assists in the development of skill acquisition and is an important aspect of any physical fitness programme. Many of the world's greatest athletes employ progressive resistance principles in their training.

1. Although weight training is great fun because you can see and take pride in the progress you are making, to become an expert still takes time—time spent on understanding and mastering each step before moving on to the next. *Don't try to run before you can walk.*
2. Before trying new exercises or training plans and schedules get and follow advice from your teacher or coach.
3. *Never train alone,* always have one stand-in at each end of the bar. *Stand-in should know what you are going to do and when.*
4. Keep to your schedule of exercises. Do not advance to poundages without your coach's advice. *Do not sacrifice correct body position for poundage.*
5. Do not try to keep up with others who may seem to be making more rapid progress than yourself. Train at your own level and within your own capabilities. *You will make progress.*
6. Horse play and practical jokes can be very dangerous. *If you are not getting enough fun out of serious weight training, it's a poor programme* Wear firm training shoes and warm clothing.
7. Check all apparatus before use and after eac exercise. Check collars. Make sure they are firml secured. Make sure all bars are evenly loaded *Concentrate and be safety conscious.*

## Important Addresses in Weight Training

**B.A.W.L.A. General Secretary and Coaching Secretary**
W. W. R. Holland, 3 Iffley Turn, Oxford.

**B.A.W.L.A. School Secretary**
D. Mulkerrin, 36 Amesbury Road, Hanworth, Middlese

**Schoolboys' Award Scheme Registrar**
H. Price, 35 Lynn Road, Terrington St. Clement, King Lynn, Norfolk.

**B.A.W.L.A. National Coach**
J. Lear, The Willows, 4 Ford's Heath, Shrewsbury.

For details of weight-training courses, further advic on weight training, details of all clubs and divisions the B.A.W.L.A., contact the B.A.W.L.A. secretar W. W. R. Holland.

## Acknowledgements

A. Murray, National Coaching Adviser, B.A.W.L.A.
G. Kirkley, Photographs (Strength Athlete)



J. Ward, Dewsbury, England